Rises In The East

A Book of Poetry

By

Ryan Fredric Steinbeck

Rises In The East

First Printing

ISBN: 978-0-578-13731-5

Acknowledgements And Thanks:

Thanks to Cindy, for constant inspiration.
Thanks to family, friends, and artists who
continue to inspire me in the both the
smallest and most substantial ways.

Thanks to Cindy for the photos

Thanks to Michael Steinbeck for the
illustration and covers.

To The Reader

Over the past two years I've focused on what I suppose is the key to survival in writing, telling stories through the eyes of others. There are many standalone poems in this collection. But the poems about love attempt to follow a progression of one character, likely a younger man, as he finds his way. Additionally there are a string of poems from a character who loses a loved one and eventually progresses toward acceptance. Bringing these characters to life has been emotionally rewarding for me as I viewed situations from a perspective other than my own. I hope it can provide a measure of reward, or resolve, for you as well.

Table Of Contents:

Table Of Contents:

To Edwin, in memoriam

Rises In The East

An emergence of textured fog
Armed to the heavens with density
Glimpsing in haze the horizon
A shipping vessel materializes
Charging through padded walls
Betraying tranquil waters

A familiar lifting
Ill favored, but my own
I must be undeserving
As she grants my amnesty

The river and its barren rage
Become traveling companions
As they're lost at the estuary
Free of restraint

Time and tide waits for no one
The sea is limitless and fitful
An observer of empirical decline
A supporter of resurrection
A foreteller of both

Beyond my own tales of loss
The river and the ocean
Shall together thrive
As I remember the time before her
When I fell

The exception proves the rule
Through the course of water
The gravity of purpose

Unaffected by present day forces
Or the reaches of history
The river always discovers the sea
The sun always rises in the east

Sun

She forms after the flood
With anxious eyes examining
And a restless mind roaming
Too long a subterranean life
Her patience derisive
Waiting to surface
To visualize the morning
Prophesized in her dreams

After a bland pseudo-afterlife
She closes the mineshaft
To collapse the endless tunnels

She cited all he wasn't
As if hers is highest reckoning
Laying outposts to his previous version
Until he fell from sight

Shadows claim the ground
Beneath rolling clouds
Her world view pivots again
With eyes fixated aloft
An eternity of optimism insurrected

She settles her odds with the darkest night
Restages a reclamation of the first hour
As the last of the ruins are burned
At the coastline the first flame of fire
Witnessed for the first time on earth
She believes in the sum of all miracles
When she sees the sun

From Nothing

I am only recent
Without time immemorial
A flock of thoughts in a gathered mind
A bleeding heart

As I shut the door
When the lock clicked
The borders of ice melted
From my frozen mind
Frozen heart
Frozen feet
I announced my absolution
From your frozen society

You knew only of standing still
I wasn't granted freedom to move
It was never impossible
Just unknown, uninformed
So I declared I came from nothing
From no one

Now the avenue clears of snow
All roads reopen
I'm beyond these surroundings
And counterfeit allowances

Fear not
You will always have your memories
Your photographs
Who you knew and loved
Is a long vanished ghost

You could consider me deceased
But the truth is the opposite
Since the memory of your face evaporated
Like rain on a summer day
It's like I've just taken my first breath

You're New Here, So We Brought Beer

As usual we attempt to be cordial
Though we're gorgeously misanthropic
Please accept this house warming gift
Even though it was an afterthought

Spurious smiles and laughter
Insults resembling compliments
I have it down to a science

Part of the epidemic and anesthesia
That certain things make them whole
Friends with similar interests
Dogs, cats, birds, kids
But we don't need who we are
To be justified or reinforced

We've perfected forged smiles
Been subtle about checking the time
At the slightest thread of interest
We refrain from elaboration
Offering a parting gift in explanation
That "you're new here, so we brought beer"
And we leave it at that

As If

For this hodgepodge of a gathering
On this quiet night
I'm guessing she knew the outcome
From my first actions and words
The way she dismissed my offerings
As if she just tasted
The blandest of courses
I was soured by the soured look on her face

Before she went inside
She'd already secured an escape route
As if I was just born yesterday
She claimed to be having a good time

The blanks are filled in
With a fools optimism
As soon as words leave my mouth
I don't recognize the man speaking
The pathetic one liners and pick up attempts
I was actually impressed
By the mountain of embarrassment
Climbed in one night

I'm that one in the corner
With no sense of self
Blaming the masses
For the issues I own

A snap shot of human nature
Nobody speaks a word
If you can't see it yourself
Then it's what you deserve
It's as if I wrote the reference book
On all the ways to be ignorant
Then narrated it with such genius

Ode To Keeping Your Mouth Shut

A long week concludes
As the ambitious, overconfident, associate
Offers sneering words in a gathering
Juvenile, explosives
Detonating seconds apart
Lacking cerebral attributes
For discerning liability
A subject change among peers
Suggests it isn't over

A combustion of impulse
You're ready to respond
At that moment you see yourself
That part that's suffered
It begins to make sense
Why you didn't get a call from a friend
Who you blamed for not keeping in touch
In this rattletrap of youth
Lies an exuberance of falsehoods
Delusions by stimulus
That you had to let damage you
Before the mending could begin

You can only hope his true friends
Are forgiving by nature
Though some aren't that fortunate
So you grit your teeth and smile
As you reluctantly order another round
The designated curfew nears
It will all be over soon

I Might As Well Have Fur

I'm all in for you
With no mutual admiration society
I'm unsure why

In doses
I fill fractions of elements
I beg at your periodic table

I look to secure the weight force
From partials of past crimes
Self-flattery to self-mockery
Returning for reckoning
I circle three times in the corner
Before I lie down

I airmail clues of disenchantment
Your disinterest a disappointment
Years of emotional water boarding
Subliminal conditioning
I now respond to one word commands
Often even hand signals
Or ringing bells

At first I couldn't bear the concept
I wanted to run
To be free from caged thought
Despite my flimsy backstory
Or feeble escape attempts
I came to rely on it
As I'm chained in your backyard
This has become my only delusion
My eventual final resting place
I might as well have fur

Props And Backdrops

The frozen cerebral twilight
Driving, horizontal rain
It scatters, then restarts
Ice accumulated on my stony path

I was the frown on faces
All the deficits and humiliation
A misfire of potent impurity
A disruption to logic in a thinkers world
The tailwind of violence
In a time of passive thought

Though I was exclusively seasonal
Like the rays of the sun
You warmed the skin
Affecting the imagery outside my head

You've become my only mission
Everything cascades around you
Like props and backdrops
In support of the main theme
A plot self-sustaining
With cables detached

All other dimensions closed
Access portals shut down
Shipping lanes abandoned
I am here now
To begin again for the last time

Staring Out The Window Into The Woods

Staring out the window into the woods
Far from the maddening crowd
She endeavors to settle on a solution
The provisions failed in the space arranged
She rummages the atmosphere of alternatives
Perhaps she yearns to be the wilderness
Never deprived of purpose
If I hadn't been so reckless
She may have already found a way out

A whistle blows in the township
She shifts her stance slightly
Anchoring her efforts for another year
Determined to unearth a conclusion

She has yet to be rewarded
For her soul's incompatibility
She remains because that's who she is
With command of countenance she lives unseen
A formidable affliction has been building
In a place once filled with confidence

Remembrance of a transient optimism
In the corners of structure
Where cracks receive light
She knows departure and resolve awaits
Drawing a smile from the depths

Staring out the window into the woods
I could exhume my entire vocabulary
At the end of the day that would be futile
As she is beautiful beyond words

Alive

I want my substance to be significant
Like freefall I want to begin
To feel the freedom of passion

My offerings are my own
I'll run my own distance
Without broadcasts or praise
I won't sit at another's table
Listening to faltering disciples

I deny recommendations
I choose my own favorite wine
I will lead and not follow
Forgive not forget
So let me be
Let me think for myself
My purpose is in passage
To be channeled and serene
I am every moment ahead
And every second by
I don't need to be told I'm alive

In This Predicament

A new beginning in my head
As the old one begins to fray
This mirage still exists
Believable to everyone else
But I know you can tell
By the inflection in my voice

In this new predicament
With you
As we lie broken
Weathered, wandered
Crooked in shape
Invisible to the outside world
Simultaneous fear and laughter
If voices are used
Or cards are shown
The worlds around us
Crumbled, demolished
Banishment, exoneration
Excommunicated, exiled
Into a state of unknown
A beautiful spiral
Of detrimental proportions
Unforgiven, no return

So when do we begin?

After Death

So it was said
I promised
You swore
The court official presided
Friends and family witnessed

The beginning of the start
An immeasurable agreement
It lasted long enough for me to believe
It would always last

The comfortable ambiances
Adversaries scavenging truces
The lack of arguments
Complacency the visitor
I built a room in the back for it to stay

Yours a revisionist's history
Color to black and white
My lack of spiritual wealth
Never would have bothered you
Had it not been for my loss of riches

So it goes how it did
Consumed by empty spaces
The unforeseen unpreparedness
Cuts across the grain
Giving way to the changing of guards
As I shape shift
Hopeful for intergalactic relevance
I lose sight of the ground below

Stifled by shortness of breath
Like another new start
We vowed until death do we part
This must be after death

Proclivity

I believe in believing
So I chased my fears
Back to the source town
When I was unequivocally royal
A night watchman
Reincarnation of fear
I needed the action
I hadn't the words
Reinforcement, repercussion
Heralded, I was
Or so I thought
Until what I perceived as physical gifts
Began to betray me
Admiration wilted
As vanity blossomed

I dismissed them as useless and shallow
But it must've been me
The patient admirers
Offering opportunities
None of them I accepted
I blamed the weather and obligations
On the decline in numbers
Until they dwindled to nothing
This is what I amount to
I didn't want to fight with confidence
Or give the stage to shame
Unable to hone a single thought
Why so many voices in my head?
When my proclivity is to silence

Stagehand

Each night I have a front row seat
Every line you recite is directed at me
That's what I tell myself
I relate when you speak of kings
And decrees of punishment to commoners
Workers condemned for defiance
Penalties undefined in vocabulary
In this carousel of feelings
I believe every line

When the curtains close
You congratulate the cast and crew
With loved ones close at hand
A simple glimpse in my vicinity
Through noncommittal eyes

The after party
You're more glowing than ever
This is your biggest night
He says he loves you the most
As he stands in the distance
Too consumed with the supporting cast
To understand the milestone you surpassed
So I reserve space next to you
Acknowledging the words he missed
Ingenuity is not in my nature
But I was on cue tonight
Rewarded by the grace of your smile
The weight of the moment carried you
For the first time we found each other
No more barriers
Our eyes met without hesitation
As the congregation winds down
I know there is more to our play
Even though I'm just a stagehand
I think you fell in love with me tonight

Gain and Loss

I had no tangible assets
To ascend this mountain of approval
Roaming through seasons of dispersion
With nothing of worth to prove

We look to the same sky
We see different stars
I'd be lying if I didn't say
I wished there were moments
When your tunnel vision turned panoramic
I might be foolish to ever think it could

Sometimes I miss what could've been
Though I don't know what it feels like
The sound of this silence in my head
Is the resultant peace I've found instead

It's not within you to understand
You'd have to step outside
Simple in theory yet unviable to actualize
Still well worth the gain and loss in the end

To The Old Version

You speak of darkness
Preach about light
As if a child has a new toy
As if the words owe you something
Like a purveyor

In this dream world
You're a rock star
Without the music
Or hard work

You'll come to know in time
Not everything is a perfect rhyme
But you looked to impress
Not to connect
You failed to treat moments
As if they could be the last

An owner of nothing
Often silence would be the better choice
And knowing where you'll land
Before you leap

Composite of Grey Times

Come down from your girders
Away from hearts of steel
They've overthrown your colonies
Let your wings guide you east
Nest within our confines
You'll never have to leave

They who are old in philosophy
Cater to majority rule
Burying compassion in time and numbers
A composite of grey times outlasts their hope
For fear of revealing a soft side
If they had worked in your favor
You would still have a home

Allow the dust from the rubble to clear
The destruction be your past
Clear your repetitive mind and memory
Move into green meadows and tall trees

That which is precious and innocent
That which is worth protecting
A man out of touch with the world never sees

Breathing Room

At the forefront of this tempest
We are two shapeless entities
The winds of anonymity dance between us
The shadow grows to substance
Angel wings with dragon scales

You are too forgiving
Blunt force with steady hands
Innocently woven together
I remain to rectify

I crawl to the altar
Across the temple floor
Séances awaken old ghosts
Rising from dungeons
Passing through me
Terrorizing one last time
I am pulverized to opaqueness
Free of all husks
Flattened and hollowed
Ready to be filled
Love once the enemy of my harvest
I try to push the walls
For breathing room
But it doesn't circumvent
It retains its nature
So I accepted

It does no good
To chase love in echoes
But to find confined spaces
Trace the melody
For in it is nothing and everything
Left for it to decide if willing
I become a part of it
Not it of me

When the truth of me stands forth
Seeds will be sewn
Silences will return
The light will bend in my favor
The heart will praise the failures
That left me for ruin
And delivered me to this moment

The Language of Astrologers

It's not in our compositions
To run through streams and fields
Holding hands, laughing
Above the sorrow of the world
As if there are scriptures
Or ancient texts
On how to prove our feelings
Because we're not fathers or mothers
We don't strive for white picket fences
Or believe in delusions of normalcy
That rarely ever flourish

We don't want to be a part of research
On how to control raw energy
That removes the emotion
Then wonder how we failed

When it's set free
When it finds what it's seeking
It will settle
Morphing into what they tried to make it
Maybe those that survive
Are those that let go
Trusting the heart

If this is the result of study
All the reasons for questioning sanity
If this is what's written in the stars
Then I have no interest in reading it

In the Absence

I traveled far to arrive
These new regions
The rain caught up with me
At the overrun fields
The castles we relied upon
Now abandoned
I prepared a meeting of the minds
One side didn't show
So I unlocked the door

The excess speed was unstated
Returning from lower apsis
Neighbors pretend nothing followed
As the stain of the region
Condemned and neglected
Swiftly burned to the earth

I calmly made my distance
Never once looking back
The origin undetectable
The analysis an exercise in futility
No suspects ever named

I couldn't just leave it there
With so many demons lurking
Embraced in the absence of exorcism
As the wind scales back
Fossilized secrets now embers

I switched vehicles at the interchange
Passing sirens wailing
In the opposite direction
I watch the last of the smolder
Over the tree tops many miles away

Leave The Conversation

We assemble often
Clichés and clans
Demanding our customary spaces

Seldom branching out
Mindful of borders
We routinely stay within ourselves

I try to listen
As you speak of conquest, domains dominated
I search myself for admiration
I just can't seem to find any

You bask beneath every light
Only exposing insecurities
Sentinels of interest change
No one wants to watch your parade

A tedious cycle
You float to the surface
Fall to the depths
Emerging with a new polished item
No exit strategy

I imagine all of this
As I pretend to listen
Conjuring up excuses to leave the conversation
To recharge my patience
So I can endure the repeat presentation

Basket Case

I sketched a circle and hid inside
I coveted it that way for a long time
Content in refuge's binding
Not to speak for loss of words

I loved who I wanted to be
Not what I became
I didn't want what I accrued
At the expense of what I'd lost
I gave myself to the cause
Before the disclaimers
Denoting all the sacrifices
I think I skipped a step
Maybe a decade's worth of time

As the cowboys cheer
The hostesses host
I'm at the epicenter of a story I didn't write
Firing at temptations from the devil
After a consultation with reflection
A conversation with remorse

I offer a truce
The only way I survive
Freezing outlooks in their state of joy
Hoping one day I'll return
Until then I'll remember what it was like
As I stay inside my circle
Just outside the emotional sphere
Emitting all the signals
Crying out for help
Confronting anyone who breaches my border

The Line

Overhead lights dim
Garland hangs low from the ceiling
Dirty plates stacked on tables
Lipstick smeared on glasses

In the corner, a conversation
Kicking the past out of time
To photos when they stood together
United in secret
She discovered she was on the outside
Looking in at fairy tales
Foundations of a shattered dream
Essence of missed opportunity
Moments trapped in her head
Drowning in fathoms of dishonesty

She dismisses it as inheritance
Every face is recycled
Every act a plot against her

It's difficult to reminisce
When the surface of good is broken
Lines begin to fade
Often a one way road to obscurity
When you're already half a ghost
When pain's threshold is no longer recognizable
It could be time to draw the line

Buried in the adaptation of guilt
He reaches out of the shallows
Unable to take a breath
Steering through her stifling stronghold

Not worth the tax on his soul
He's not the object of this downfall
Or a solution to enduring narratives
Of a life on the edge of nihilism
Emerging from self-preservation
He had to draw the line

North Side Of Birmingham

There are things I remember
What I've been told
A catharsis in crime
From an outside force
My dispute was with the devil, son
Not with you

In the middle of a laugh
My mind trailed off on a tangent
To a far distant time
When I let the bottle dictate
Who I was
Who would see you grow

I tried to splice together
The strands of my attributes
Most of them too frayed
To stand on their own

A body weak with dishonor
On eroded pillars of shale
Washing away in southern tide
As I watch the sunset fade

I let my eyes wander
I watched my makings scatter
Like an apparition on display
The last of my visions was you

Time forced its way
Onto the splicing table
Where I'd hoped to cut out the middle
I wanted a place in the world
To secure a space in the afterlife
But I didn't possess the dialogue

When you found me, forgave me
On the North side of Birmingham
You retold stories of a man
Who would help me believe
I could be saved
As in Capernaum or Gennesareth
Cultivating enough to lay my head
On the bed of eternity

Finally free of my bones
My fate now in another's hands

A Rainy Day Remembers

A rainy day remembers
A busy subway
A smile from a stranger
As I shared her space
I don't remember a name or face
I stumbled into a conversation
A range of politics
I had no interest debating
She did, so I pretended

She bounced her words off of me
I was more than amenable
I guess I was lonely
Strong, sharp observations
Enduring until they called our stop
Platform 16
I wasn't prepared for the rain
We shared her umbrella
As she continued to assert her aggravations
I just as well could've been a mute
Unsure how so much time had passed
We parted ways at Southport Avenue
I claimed that my focused mind
Had other obligations

Every night, for a week, maybe two
I passed her flat
Hoping I might catch her
But the city won this one
I never saw her again
I'm still not sure if it was love
I think I just needed a friend

Explode

A deep inhale
Waiting
A slight tinge
A small flair of color
Still the summer refused to let go
September rolled over
Turning blue in the face
Until the mid-October rains
Fought for the long overdue
Even when the fight wasn't fair

As the puddles multiplied
The mid-year sun's ambition waned
From its prolonged unwelcome stay
Realizing the inevitable
Deciding to give way

The state of affairs collapsed
The morning brought a welcomed feel
Without a mourning for days passed
The memorial was brief
The exhale, long
As the colors exploded into fall

Musings Of A Self-Proclaimed Genius

I decided I was the genius and the rebel
I ratted out God and logic
I condemned my affiliations
At both ends of the spectrum
While I polished my debate skills
All is fine as long as I'm right
And I know you're wrong
I'm here to offer proof
Of the fraudulence of preachers
Followers and their misfortune
Neither experiences have I shared
Most likely never will
In my rich tapestry of life
I've never been forced to own the pre-owned
Or accept hand-me-downs

I will hack away at your perspective
Give you a world of suggestions
I will scoff and ridicule undetected
You'll thank me for it eventually
If you ever reach my pedestal

The Unruly Bunch

In the summer's duration
A stillness ruled
A revolving door of feathery beings
Our offerings an afterthought

But an unseasonal cold ignited fears
Disorienting compasses
Of an unruly bunch
Starlings, grackles, blackbirds

Casual visitations regressed
To a gathering festival of feasting
Similar to our own
But the regulars turned defensive
Fighting for their shares

Trapeze artists on twigs
Awkward poses
Diving to the ground
Challenging the pecking order

Maybe they have a language
Or give each other names
Look down on one another
Curse each other

Soon it's closing time
Last call of the afternoon
Gone like the wind, they are
In a matter of moments

A Better Time

I arrive with the arctic winds
Belongings in tow
My vision blurred by an argument
Declared as a conversation

I shake beads of water from my hat
This dry morning will quench the thirst
In the shallow spaces of laughter
Between my weighted thoughts

I've waited like this before
Between here and there
Eventually the Westbound arrives
Engulfed by a thousand eyes of worry
Self-absorption is an ally today
So no one provides an accurate account
Should they ever be asked

I'm not looking to harm
I just want a better life
I can't do that with you around
We were the origin of inevitability

Painted pictures in my head
Water colors dance in light
Chrysanthemums remind me of the balcony
Where we once had my favorite conversation
That not everything has to make sense

May there be discovery
May it be your heart's journey home
To the true uninhabited soul you lost
The one you always could've been
There isn't a better time
Nor a better place
To forgive

Forever In A Day

Since we can't start over
I'll wish for an ability
To spin the world backward
Tomorrow would be the day
We said goodbye for good
It will improve from there

Those awful things I did
Before you realized
All the flaws in this system
The spiteful things you said
In response
Will be forgotten and erased

Soon we're a step closer
To when you moved home
To expunging your confession
That you never loved me

Further on we'll forget
Minds moving into darkness and obsession
The doom and dread about facing days
We'll get back to the beginning
When you could look my way
A beginning that would now be our ending
Our happy ever after
I will try to stop the world there
Live forever in that day

Maybe In The Next Life

These photos
From a short while ago
I remembered you in that time
The sad exhausted eyes
I held the magnifying glass
Up to your pale skin
Pretending to be a man who didn't love you
For the woman you would be
Before and after me
I'm arrested in remembrance
Every time we are close
Nonchalantly brushing hands, shoulders
Portrayals of innocence
Neither of us feels
These are the roles we're playing
The character identities we've assumed
We don't relinquish hope it could change
Or the fear to change it

Inside this weakness
There's a great deal of strength
Neither of us possess
So as we look in each other's eyes
Into a lifetime of scenarios
None we will wish on the world
We'll abandon the belief in alternatives
As the sinking moon tells the truth
As light drenches peaks and valleys
Decisions are made and enforced
Silently we decide to do no harm
Maybe in the next life
We'll see what happens then

Outdated Format

I'm reaching out
If only to tell you
I won't be requesting your presence
On the grounds of this house of pain
Nor to be a character in this horror story

That portion is now destitute
A cancer in remission
So please know I come here
With an unseen past and redacted history
And new building blocks

I don't need you any closer
I just didn't want you further away
The imagery of our movie
Is on an outdated format
I don't need a sequel
I just wanted to tell you
I'm thinking of you
And I'm sorry

Silent Partner

Rewind to the dark ages
Fast forward
Still the monsters found a way
To overshadow the rational choice
The better half

A will forced
By threat of retaliation
That was the way they reigned

Children in all corners
Violence as the first action
Violence begetting violence
While the silent partner wakes from slumber
Looks on with disgust
Holds her tongue
Waiting her turn

Often we seem a separate species
The gaping hole of dichotomy
Inclinations to destroy
Regression over comfort

She observes the pitfalls
Missed opportunities
Sometimes inaction is action
Information gathering
Over target practice
Someday a revolution
Our order of importance
Will course correct
An enormous step forward
Toward true achievement

At The Shallow Bay

My introductory sequence
Distinguished and animated
Blown to pieces
Mostly lost
But survived in fragments
Enough preservation
To construct in the same location

I conspired
Revolting in time
Leaving the village mid-growth
Still impressionable
To retaliatory expeditions
A refugee among the people

My insurgence gained strength
As a designated separatist
From a declining system
My value continued to rise

In search of solace
I find a cabin at the shallow bay
Here I will live my life's term
In the silent current of water

She found me
By the evidence I left behind
Only she could decipher

Other possessions fleeting
I'm sorry this isn't want you envisioned
Just know I don't blame you anymore
This is precisely where I'm supposed to be

Slow

I carry your locket
Your face a reminder
Don't always operate at high speed

I crawl to the next opening
It devours me
The time required
For the mundane

These methods are obsolete
I'm speaking through glass
Mouth moving, no words
Then, as with sound delay
It reaches you
Though all for naught
I hear the echo on the other side

So I'm left with noise
You call sounds
Excuses you call explanations
But really all my frustrations
Are lodging complaints
About being lodged in a slow vice

An ear to the ground
The rhythm of the world
Message sent and received

It is I
The exception
To unwritten rules
Still unforgiving
I do welcome this pace
But it's another kind of slow
That is sought

May Cause Miracles

I have long refused shelter
Sanctioning shadowy forces
Attempting to stand firm
On slippery slopes

Battlements were assembled
Keeping you at a distance
Never questioning the literature
Suggesting you were wrong

Charge with the battering ram
In lieu of negotiation
No wisdom to reference
Or skills to polish

Then, sudden darkness
Irrigation of faith runs out
Bones are tested
Frustration abates with reality
These nights will be longer than ever

I seek meaning beyond mirrors
A voice that breaks barriers
Engaging the art of trust
Turning of the hourglass
A redefined philosophy
To reflect the new choice of combat
I could've resisted until the end
But sooner the end would come

If I find the soul of a stranger
Confess to a diary
That I may not be faultless
Then it may cause miracles
That I can recall one day
In my elders chair
With the fire of reflection before me

Death's Trial Run

I've seen this before
The way the snow is falling
Soon a major change in the story
The lights flicker on
Revealing a path
Onto the bridge to heaven
A piece of me awaits there, wondering
Soon to be lost

By just being here, being you
You helped me
Through the bleakness
You were a time consuming obligation
I'd give the world to keep
You were comfort
A peaceful ambiance

Knowing how the world would be without you
I already miss you
The secrets of tomorrow yet revealed
Though I recognize the unavoidable

You consume my thoughts
We won't do well without the other
You're eyes are one hundred voices
You've fought valiantly for a long time
Maybe it's time to surrender

I just want you to know
How thankful I am for you
How much better you made my life
If you have the capacity to reflect
Then I hope at the end of your time here
I will have done the same for you

Presence

There's something different
About the harvest moon on this eve
The wind gusts must've been a warning
The change in gravitational pull
It was something I didn't realize I knew
I hadn't acknowledged or accepted
Until it was too late
The plan was for a storybook ending
To be conscious of the signs
To know the last thing I'd say to you

Where do you go?
Where do I focus my energy
When I speak to you?
I hope in your new place
You'll construct your own living space
Build the framing of heaven's gates
As a smile returns to your face
For the tethers are released
Nagging earthly human ordinances
No longer apply
What remains are the essentials
The love you give and take with you

As word travels fast
Our hearts grow heavy
Eyes tell their stories
Embraces last a little longer
Though the mind seeks vocabulary
The right thing to say
When the truth is there is none
No handbook or dialogue
That could ever make a difference

What lies in fundamental pattern
The temperance and adhesive
Unique in this day and age
Is that which has always defined us
At the end of a long journey
Accompanied by souls departed
Gone but not forgotten
The only trophy on the mantel is presence
All we have is each other

The Same House

I cast away these stones into the river
That grows wide just beyond the bend
A stone's throw from the passage grave
Where final words were written and said

I bridge the distance between belief and fear
On the opposite bank the chime of church bells
As the river flows without stopping
I hope I didn't tumble aimlessly through time
Landing devoid of purpose

For all I am is right here
There is no before or after
It's as if there never was

To the left of me, new development
To the right, a building in ruins
I need to decide which direction to face

I've become alienated by interpretations
Of forgiveness and acceptance
This doesn't feel like the same house
Defined in the scriptures
That comforted me through the years
Rejoicing through observance
Of all the simple things
While strangle holding the sorrow
It's so difficult to term this a new beginning
When all of my stones have been thrown
Here's to a better tomorrow

Such Little Distractions

In these waning hours of the waxing crescent
I wish to reverse the course of time
To a time when I didn't realize
I wouldn't live forever

I give way to every day disruptions
Accelerating the unavoidable
While slowing the nourishment of the soul

I have an urgency to become something
To live more than I have
It's a waste to waste hours
On such little distractions

To be buried in the vastness of emptiness
Creating a scheme for a head on collision
With the ending of your time
That you won't see coming
Unless you alter barometric readings

It's more than statements
Than saying you only live once
It's not about indignation
It's about joy and celebration

Edwin's Hymn

The hour has come to rest
This body weakened by trials of time
My tapestry is taken down
Weaved into the firmament
With patience I wait in the crossing

I am here to witness
The last of the mysteries
The passage of release
The memory of me as it lives in you
The exhale blankets you
Carries on in wind and waves
Protecting and keeping you

Let me be lifted
Help my soul be received
Let me know I've done enough
To enter your sanctuary
Be still and your time will near, he says
Succumb to the beautiful calm
To the absence of time

I feel the forgiveness flow over me
Rowing into all of my vessels
As I come to know why I believed
Sorrow carries and reforms
Pollinating goodwill for the left behind
Channeling the sanguinity
To the souls still trapped in bodies
They will know I've arrived
They will know what's waiting
Not just to believe
To be alive
To prepare your way
Deliver the peace you carry
As your wandering acquaintance

Don't rush
Stay and give what you can
When the time does come
I'll be waiting at the gates for you

Limited Number

I maneuver through the squall
The morning fatigue
Finding myself entranced
By the smallest of sentiments
Realizing my tenure on this soil
Has an unknown expiration date

To look ahead, a death sentence
To look behind, treason
To be here as minutes pass
Will keep me tethered to this shoreline

So I change colors
I limit the number of frowns to be seen
I hold my glass up to history
Let the angels fall where they may
We should attempt to be who we are
Who we imagine ourselves to be
There are only so many occasions to waste
And a limited number of days to celebrate

Train of Thought

I ride rails
Out of the blue aftershock
In my train of thought

That was the last stop
So I move on to the next
No use dwelling
At crossroads already crossed

The morning light
These lines another day deeper
The leaves one more day turned
With the cold weather approaching

I arrive at my final beach
I see the setting sun
My feet are in the sand
But still moving

The Storm That Never Was

From here I can see the end of the front
Where warm meets cold
Ice particles suspended as shapes
Past and future crystalized inside
If anything were to happen
It would happen here

Therein lies anticipation and wonder
I huddle and brace
For what is leading, following
There's a measure of both
I'm underneath the paradox
The chain of clouds one million miles high
The blasphemy echoes
From a far off distant place
The turbulence of the oncoming disturbance
Withdraws into the atmosphere

The earth and its sky
Simultaneously exhale
Taking back the angry warning, for now
As the first rays of the morning sun
Appear on the other side

Within the Space

Vapor trails in cross section
A light brush of paint for the clouds
Ordering the morning moon to fade
Into the purest blue of the day

If only once in a while
I'd like to be at peace
Without the consequence of modern times
In dark escape masquerading as reward

I question the significance of necessities
Forcing loss of interest
To leave this viewpoint behind
Move to the less essential
When the entire reason to persevere
Is right here before me

If you find your way back to earth
Please implement my plans for reform
It was once such a simple thing to be loved
Within the space of a lifetime
The hardest part should be turning away

Bay of Mortality

Turning corners to a sun drenched embankment
Saying goodbye is never easy
A commute across the bay
Morning midst rising
The river's bend rips open a new landscape
Waking long docile molecules
Ready to accept the changing drift

Shivering cold
An understanding of what's ahead
The commitment
The undertaking
Wishing the space to decide
Was expanded instead of condensed
That I could maneuver inside these hours
So they would feel like years
To not have fear
Of the diminished water level
In this bay of mortality

Even in the absence of rain
Lights flicker through the fog
I decode a message
I am at the mercy of the unknown
The uncontainable
Still the answers will be forthcoming
As long as eyes scan the horizon
It goes on for as far as I have sight
It never ends until it starts over

Going Home

This welcome day
I traversed the North, South divide
Through federations, territories, time zones
As a force bigger than one another
United the work that had finished
With the finishing hand

You were a shelter in a time of seeking
These stars are my sleeping pills
My opium
Mesmerized by repetition
I wait for the moon's dark side
With no sand left to scatter
I lose track of time

As I focused on where I was headed
Instead of why I was leaving
We set aside our differences for this journey
Thinking and wanting the same thing
We are going home

Not Sorry Anymore

It became ritualistic
Turning back the page
Rereading, reliving
All of the times he was responsible
When he wasn't what he became yet
Several missing pieces

A nomadic journey of recovery
Details of cold arguments
Ice like fire
Burning in veins
Still there was calm in his demeanor
Sanity in his madness
Delayed realization
About how thoroughly destructive he was
In such a quiet way

Cloaks of self-deception
Draped across open spaces
A dark pit taking years to climb out
Remorse for hearts broken
Sprawled across a wasteland

It's times like these
When discoveries about resilience are born
The knowing that if you had a do over
You'd handle with better care
So in new growth
He turns in his final product
Praying to the world's ether
To heal wounds of his responsibility

With that he goes forth
With a reassembled heart
Knowing he will never falter as before
He doesn't have to be sorry anymore

Nomad

After a bridge of trust burned with lies
I proceeded north
Tall trees and blueberry fields
On both knees I dirtied my hands
Aligned myself with the rules
Tried to be thankful
The day always came
When voices weren't deciphered as words
Declared trails behind
Circle back around
In the right light there's no denial
That circumvents the truth for long
I forgive the mistress of hope
That ties me to continuance
Nourishing my psychosis
So as the welcome wagon rots and crumbles
I move on

A central city
With privileged paths to the trees
Liaisons with distinction
Dabbling in hysteria
She drinks a white wine
Introduces a new regime
I shed my outer coat
Buy into the philosophy
At the bonfire of my initiation
She takes my hand in hers
Tells me to let go of the uneasy feeling
To hold my feet still
To learn the safety of this love
I'm a nomad no more

Sometimes

Sometimes I'm surprised by the sky
I want to change shape
Be the air
Dissolve into the troposphere

Now and then I'm reassured
By unexpected smiles of those passing
This compassion a diamond in the rough

At times the elegance on display
By a mother to a child
Is all I need to move on from the day

Sometimes a touch of a hand
On a cold evening
When the turning stars
Fight their destiny
Is the warmest of all possibilities

Every time you come into focus
There is nothing more
Than the fullness of my heart
That is the reason for everything
All that I am

Within

I greet the world in morning
With the greatness of silence
Of early rising emergence
The sleeping sun
Not yet friends with the horizon

The pause between breath
Seemingly much larger
The vacation of thought for a moment
I'm closer to finding what I am
In these opportunities
Tiny gifts of benevolence
Like an explosion, then implosion

So far from unknowing, uncaring
And not listening
So close to an ending monumental storyline
That had its turn
Now it's time to conclude

I know of many arguments about solutions
Rights and wrongs
I also know everything that is possible
Every outcome
All comes from within

Without

All these grand gestures
Of upright thought
Of waves
Without paddles
Or swimming devices
An end where dreams lie
But don't lie still
For a moment passes
Like the present to past
Like birds flying south
Like scuttling
Conversion in equipped senility
Where the truth never hurts
When you don't remember it
It's riveting from learned behavior
To donations of frail thought
As we climb to upper slopes of conviction
And wonder, and joy
Only to sometimes fall
Fall to record low temperatures
That is emptiness without love
Few prisons hold more cold futility
Few open houses hold more optimism
Than acceptance
Such a magnitude of forthcoming survival
As we stay to see the end
As we forgive
Believe
In temples
Where peace lives
Where we can flourish
Together
Always without time
Without hate
Without war
Without death

www.ingramcontent.com/pod-product-compliance
Lightning Source LLC
Chambersburg PA
CBHW032058040426
42449CB00007B/1117